WHERE WISDOM MEETS
Wonder

A Workbook of Renewal, Agency, and Direction

WONDER CRONE

By Jennifer L. Butz | WonderCrone.com

Contents

Welcome..3

The Natural Rhythm of Aging...5

Creating a Sacred Space..7

Turn #1—Embracing Our Aging...33

Turn #2—Accepting the Full Cycle of Life..38

Turn #3—Living Mindfully..43

Turn #4—Respecting Compassionately...48

Turn #5—Honoring Self..54

Turn #6—Loving Self...60

Turn #7—Appreciating Simplicity..65

Turn #8—Loving Gaia..70

Turn #9—Navigating Beliefs...75

Turn #10—Sustaining Intimacy..80

Turn #11—Showing Up..85

Turn #12—Wisdom and Wonder Ceremony.....................................90

Farewell...98

Welcome!

I am delighted that you have this workbook in your hands!

Maybe you're here because you're just curious about aging. Maybe it's because you're facing the complexities of getting older or feeling uncertain about what this life chapter holds. Maybe you're asking yourself, "What does aging really mean for me?" Or maybe, just maybe, you're looking for tools that help you link the wisdom you've built throughout your life and want to use that to inform a third chapter of wonder and meaning.

Hi! I'm Jen, founder of WonderCrone. Not so long ago, I was in that place, feeling all those confused emotions and yearning to understand my past to craft a meaningful, intentional future as I entered my 60s and beyond. Like you, I sought tools to help navigate these waters, to find a language for the emotions and thoughts swirling in my mind. My journey led me to an array of resources—from scholarly articles to goddess spirituality and even Wicca.

Yet, what I needed—a grounded, actionable, insights-based approach—remained elusive. That's when I realized I had to forge my own path, drawing on a mix of research, personal experiences, and wisdom shared by peers and older women. Finally, I folded all of that together and created this workbook. The result of this journey is what I now offer to you.

I call this approach Where Wisdom Meets Wonder. This is more than just a workbook; it's a living process, a framework to personalize and own.

Whether you choose to embark on this journey alone, with a close friend, or within a small group, the pace is entirely up to you. After all, this is your next chapter—a chapter that you are writing with intention, wisdom, and the richness of your lived experiences.

Wishing you an uplifting, insightful, and productive journey to and through your third chapter!

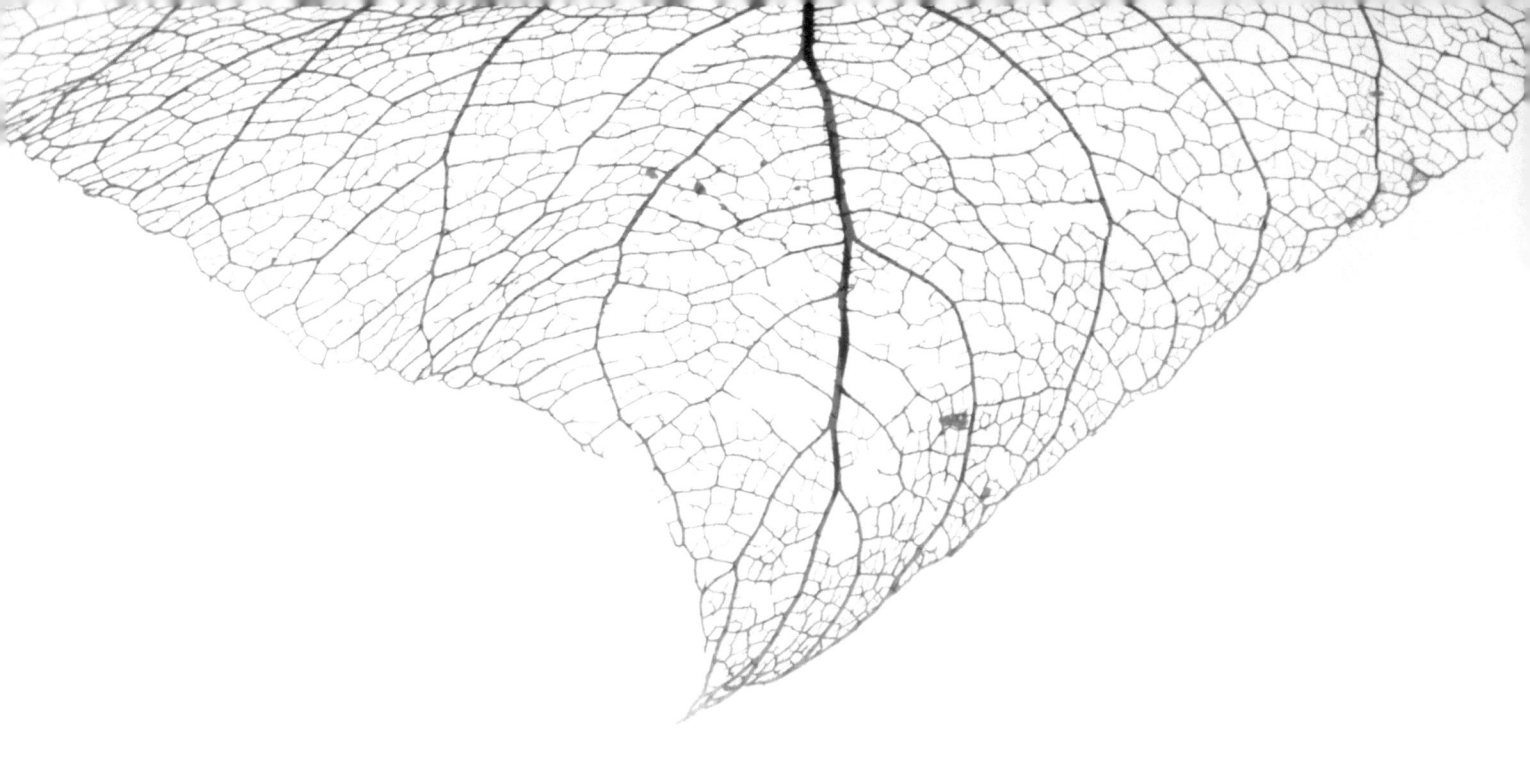

THE NATURAL RHYTHM OF AGING

Before the Abrahamic faiths overtook the world, it was widely acknowledged that a woman's life had three chapters—maiden, mother, and crone. The three phases of the moon image in the WonderCrone logo depicts each of the phases of a woman's life. Each of these chapters has power and unique roles to play in society. Today, maiden and mother are widely accepted, but "crone" has become something negative, repulsive, and even witchy. I seek to reclaim the title of crone with pride, respect, and power. This is why I named my company WonderCrone. But I realize that not everyone is on board with this – yet...

The journey into our third chapter is as natural as the changing of seasons. As The Byrds famously sang in the 1960s (drawing from Ecclesiastes 3:1-8), "To everything there is a season." This sentiment resonates deeply as we move through the phases of our lives. In keeping with this cyclical nature, each segment of this workbook is called a "Turn." There are twelve Turns in this process, each one a step on your path to deeper understanding and self-empowerment.

Each Turn follows a similar format: a brief introduction, some thoughts to ponder, questions to explore, and an intention to set. Think of each Turn as the tip of an iceberg—there's so much more beneath the surface, waiting to be discovered. Should you feel inspired to delve deeper, additional resources are provided at the end of this workbook.

Take your time with the questions in each Turn. These exercises are not about finding the "right" answers; they are about exploration. Let yourself ruminate, make decisions, and then feel free to change your mind. This is a dynamic, evolving process with no deadlines or pressure. If you find yourself asking questions that aren't listed here, add them! And if you're so inclined, share your insights with me—this is a living, breathing journey we're on together.

Each Turn concludes with an intention-setting section. I offer a suggested intention and encourage you to craft your own, aligning with your reflections and emerging sense of self.

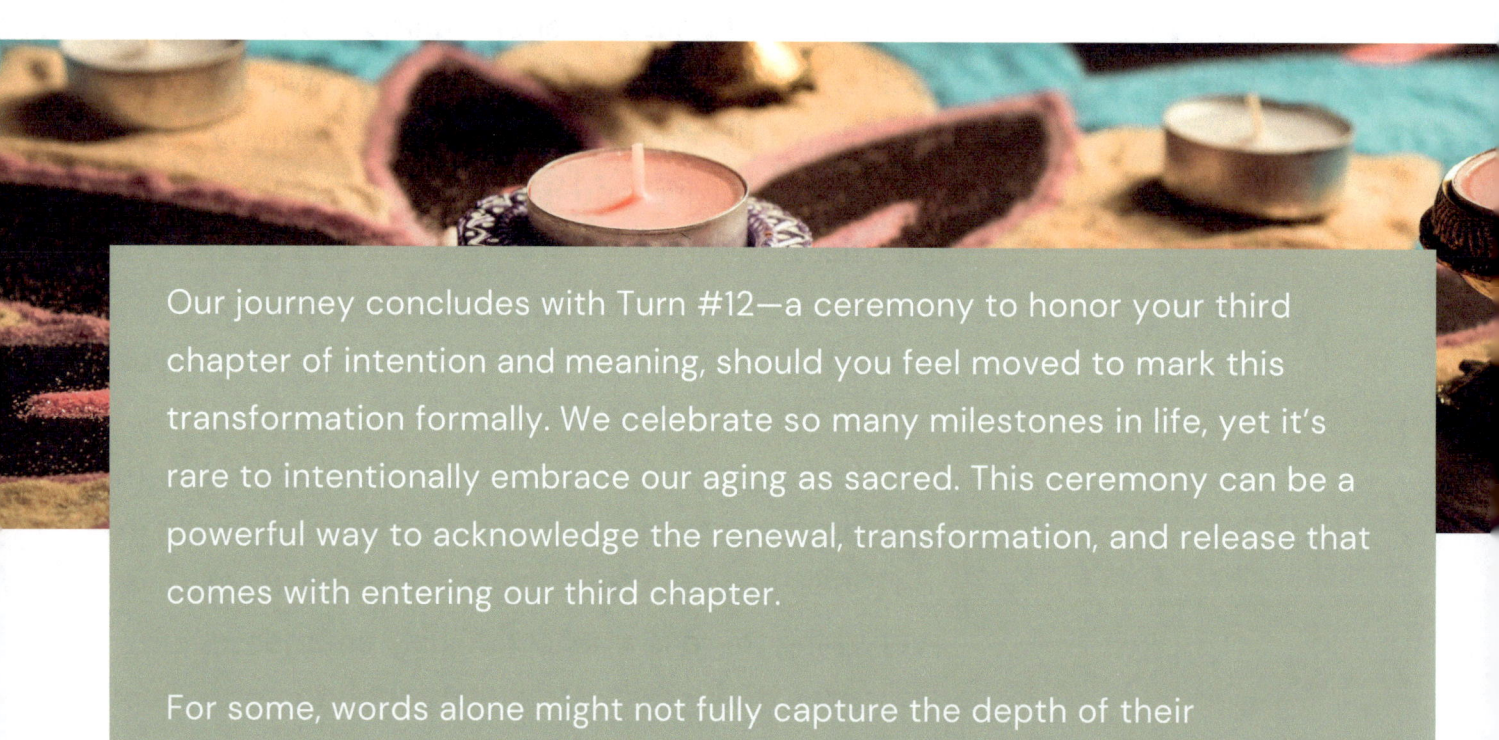

Our journey concludes with Turn #12—a ceremony to honor your third chapter of intention and meaning, should you feel moved to mark this transformation formally. We celebrate so many milestones in life, yet it's rare to intentionally embrace our aging as sacred. This ceremony can be a powerful way to acknowledge the renewal, transformation, and release that comes with entering our third chapter.

For some, words alone might not fully capture the depth of their experiences during this journey. If you find that poetry, drawing, painting, or other forms of creative expression speak to you, I encourage you to explore these avenues as well. Allow your creativity to flow as you navigate each Turn, using it as a tool for introspection and self-expression.

CREATING A SACRED SPACE

A sacred space can facilitate the journey inward, creating a sanctuary where you can retreat, reflect, and recharge. This space can be as elaborate or as simple as you wish, but what matters most is that it resonates with you and supports your wisdom and wonder journey. Statues, totems, and other altar items can play a central role in making this space sacred, imbuing it with meaning and intention.

STATUES: INVOKING THE PRESENCE OF THE DIVINE FEMININE

Statues are powerful symbols that can bring the presence of the divine into your sacred space. They can represent goddesses, ancestral figures, or other spiritual archetypes that resonate with you:

GODDESS STATUES:

A statue of Hecate, the quintessential crone goddess, might find a place on your altar. Hecate's connection to crossroads and transitions makes her a fitting guide as you navigate this new phase of life. Placing a statue of Hecate in your sacred space can help you connect with her wisdom and power, reminding you of your strength and resilience.

Other goddesses, like Demeter, representing the nurturing mother, or Persephone, symbolizing renewal and transformation, might also resonate with you. Each goddess brings her unique energy and lessons. Choose one that aligns with your current intentions or the particular Turn you're exploring.

Part of my journey has been creating mixed-media metal sculptures that I call Divine Divas. They come from across time, cultures, and geographies. Each one has a message that can lead to deeper reflection and meditation. Each Diva's story is on my website: WonderCrone.com. Feel free to explore the Divas for inspiration.

ANCESTRAL FIGURES:

For some, a statue that honors the wisdom of ancestors can be a powerful addition to the altar. This might be a representation of a grandmother or a matriarchal figure who embodies the qualities you wish to cultivate in yourself. Such a statue can serve as a reminder of the lineage of wisdom you are a part of, offering guidance and support as you reflect on your path.

TOTEMS: SYMBOLS OF PERSONAL POWER AND PROTECTION

Totems are objects that carry symbolic meaning, often representing animals, natural elements, or spiritual concepts. They are used in many cultures as tools for protection, guidance, and connection with the spiritual world. Totems might be a powerful way to anchor personal intentions and connect with deeper aspects of who you are:

ANIMAL TOTEMS

Consider incorporating animal totems that resonate with your journey into your sacred space. For example, an owl totem can symbolize wisdom and the ability to see what others do not, making it a fitting companion for reflection and insight. A wolf totem might represent the strength of the pack and the importance of community, a reminder of your support systems.

If you feel drawn to a particular animal, research its symbolism and see how it might align with your aging journey. Placing a small statue or carving of this animal on your altar can serve as a reminder of the qualities you wish to embody or call upon.

NATURAL ELEMENTS:

Stones, crystals, and shells are all potent totems that carry the energy of the earth. For example, a piece of amethyst can enhance spiritual awareness, while a seashell might symbolize the cyclical nature of life and the flow of emotions. In the following section, there is a more complete discussion about stones and crystals.

TOOLS FOR FOCUSED REFLECTION AND MEDITATION

In addition to statues and totems, other items can enhance your sacred space, helping you focus your energy and intentions:

CANDLES:

Placing a candle at the center of your altar can serve as a focal point during meditation, helping you to center your thoughts and connect with the sacred. The flame represents transformation, clarity, and the light within. Consider using candles in colors that correspond to your intentions—for example, white for purity and peace, purple for spiritual growth, or black for protection and release.

INCENSE:

Incense has been used in spiritual practices for millennia to purify the air, enhance concentration, and invoke a sense of the sacred. Choose scents that resonate with you—such as sandalwood for grounding, frankincense for spiritual clarity, or lavender for calm and peace. Burning incense as you enter your sacred space can create a ritual of transition, signaling to your mind and body that it's time to shift into a reflective, meditative state.

SMUDGING:

Smudging tools like sage or palo santo can be used to cleanse the space of negative energies, creating a refreshed environment for your spiritual work. This practice can be especially powerful before beginning a new Turn in your wisdom and wonder journey, allowing you to start each section with a clean slate. In the following section, we explore the use of herbs and spices more deeply.

SACRED TEXTS OR AFFIRMATION CARDS:

If you have a favorite book of spiritual teachings, poetry, or a set of affirmation cards, these can be valuable additions to your sacred space. Place them where they are easily accessible, and incorporate them into your daily practice by reading a passage or drawing a card for inspiration and guidance. These texts can serve as a source of wisdom and reflection, offering new insights each time you engage with them.

HEALING ENERGIES: NURTURING BODY AND SPIRIT

Many stones and gems are known for their healing properties, making them valuable allies in maintaining and restoring health. Here's how some of these stones can support your well-being:

AMETHYST:

This stunning purple stone is often associated with spiritual awareness and healing. It is known to calm the mind, ease stress, and promote restful sleep, making it an ideal stone to keep by your bedside or under your pillow. Amethyst is also believed to purify the body's energy field, removing negative influences and enhancing physical and emotional healing. As a talisman, it can be worn as jewelry or carried in a pocket to maintain a constant connection to its soothing energies.

ROSE QUARTZ:

Often called the "stone of love," rose quartz radiates a gentle, nurturing energy that can heal emotional wounds and promote self-love. It's especially powerful in matters of the heart—whether you're seeking to heal past hurts, enhance compassion, or deepen your connection with others. Placing rose quartz on your altar or carrying it with you can help open your heart chakra, encouraging forgiveness, trust, and emotional balance.

CITRINE:

Citrine is associated with prosperity, abundance, and vitality. A yellow citrine has bright, sunny energy to uplift your mood and boost your confidence, making it a great stone for overcoming depression or lethargy. Carrying citrine or placing it on your altar can help you stay motivated and focused, attracting success and positive energy into your life.

CLEANSING ENERGIES: PURIFYING AND PROTECTING YOUR SPACE

Cleansing is a crucial practice in maintaining the energetic health of both your physical space and your energy field. Certain stones are particularly effective in absorbing, transmuting, or repelling negative energy:

BLACK TOURMALINE:

This powerfully protective stone is often used to shield against negative energies, including electromagnetic pollution from electronic devices. Black tourmaline can absorb and neutralize negativity, making it an excellent stone to place near your computer or in areas where you feel vulnerable to stress or anxiety. You can also use it to cleanse your aura by holding it over your body or placing it near your root chakra during meditation.

SELENITE:

Known as the "liquid light" of crystals, selenite has an exceptionally high vibration that purifies and cleanses other stones, spaces, and your energy field. Its calming, peaceful energy makes it an ideal stone for creating a serene environment. Selenite can be used to cleanse your sacred space by placing it in the corners of a room.

CLEAR QUARTZ:

Often referred to as the "master healer," clear quartz is a versatile stone that can be used to cleanse and amplify the energy of other stones. Its ability to absorb, store, and release energy makes it a powerful tool for clearing negative energies and enhancing the properties of other crystals. Placing clear quartz in your sacred space or wearing it as jewelry can help you maintain a clear, focused mind and a purified energy field.

EMPOWERING ENERGIES: ENHANCING PERSONAL POWER AND SPIRITUAL GROWTH

Stones and gems can also serve as talismans that enhance your personal power, support spiritual growth, and help you manifest your intentions:

LABRADORITE:

This mystical stone is often associated with transformation and the awakening of one's inner magic. Labradorite enhances intuition, psychic abilities, and spiritual insight, making it an excellent stone for those who are exploring their aging and seeking to deepen their connection with the unseen world. The stone can be worn during meditation or carried with you to help you tap into your inner wisdom and navigate times of change with grace and clarity.

OBSIDIAN:

A powerful stone for protection and grounding, obsidian is often used to clear mental confusion and release negative energies from the past. It can help you uncover hidden truths, bringing subconscious patterns to the surface for healing. Obsidian is a great stone for shadow work—a process of exploring and integrating the darker aspects of yourself. Place obsidian in your sacred space or carry it as a reminder of your strength to confront and heal past traumas.

MOONSTONE:

Connected to the energy of the moon and the Divine Feminine, moonstone is a stone of new beginnings, intuition, and emotional balance. It's particularly powerful for women, as it supports hormonal balance and enhances feminine energy. Moonstone can be used during your menstrual cycle or at any time when you're feeling emotionally overwhelmed. As a talisman, moonstone can be worn as jewelry or placed under your pillow to enhance dreams and intuition.

To harness the full power of these stones and gems, consider creating a personal talisman—a piece of jewelry, a pouch, or a small bundle that you can carry with you or keep in your sacred space. Here's how you can create one:

1 CHOOSE YOUR STONES:

Select stones that resonate with your current needs and intentions. For example, if you're focusing on healing and protection, you might choose amethyst, black tourmaline, and rose quartz. If you're seeking empowerment and spiritual growth, you might opt for labradorite, moonstone, and obsidian.

2 CLEANSE YOUR STONES:

Before using your stones, cleanse them to remove any residual energy. This can be done by placing them in sunlight or moonlight, using a smudging tool like sage, or setting them on a bed of selenite for several hours.

3 SET YOUR INTENTION:

Hold your stones in your hands and close your eyes. Take a few deep breaths, grounding yourself in the present moment. Set a clear intention for how you wish the stones to support you—whether it's for healing, protection, empowerment, or another purpose. Visualize the stones absorbing your intention, filling with the energy you wish to manifest.

4 ASSEMBLE YOUR TALISMAN:

Place the stones in a small pouch, wrap them in a cloth, or string them together as a necklace or bracelet. This talisman can be carried with you throughout the day, placed on your altar, or kept under your pillow at night. Whenever you touch or see your talisman, reconnect with the intention you've set, allowing its energy to support you in your journey.

BRING IT ALL TOGETHER

Creating a sacred space with statues, totems, crystals, and other altar items is a deeply personal process. Surrounding yourself with symbols and objects that resonate with your spirit and reflect your intentions can support your journey. Whether your sacred space is a permanent fixture in your home or a temporary setup you create during your wisdom and wonder sessions, the items you choose should speak to you on a soul level.

Take your time in selecting these items, and allow your sacred space to evolve as you do. As you move through each Turn of this workbook, you might find new symbols or totems that call to you, or you might feel drawn to rearrange your space to reflect your growth and changing intentions.

Remember, this space is yours—it's a sanctuary where you can be fully yourself, free to explore, reflect, and connect with the deeper currents of life. Let it be a place of comfort, inspiration, and spiritual nourishment as you continue your journey into your third chapter.

THE ANCIENT WISDOM OF HERBS AND SPICES

In our fast-paced, technology-driven world, it can sometimes feel like ancient practices are out of step with the demands of modern life. Yet, ritual and self-care are well-known approaches to strengthening our psyche and our hearts in challenging times. The timeless power of herbs and spices offers a simple, natural way to reconnect with ourselves and the earth, even amid our busy schedules.

Herbs and spices have long been revered for their potent effects on the mind, body, and spirit. Across cultures and centuries, they've been used in rituals, medicine, and daily life to inspire, calm, rejuvenate, and heal. Their versatility and natural origins make them a timeless resource for those seeking to connect with the earth's wisdom.

Here's how you can bring these wonderful essences into your everyday life, making them part of your routine, rituals, and wisdom and wonder journey.

INSPIRATION AND MENTAL CLARITY

Herbs have been used for millennia to sharpen the mind, inspire creativity, and foster clarity. For instance:

ROSEMARY

has been a symbol of remembrance and clarity since ancient Greece. Students would weave rosemary into their hair while studying, believing it would strengthen their memory. Today, rosemary oil is still used in aromatherapy to stimulate the mind and promote clear thinking.

PEPPERMINT

has been cherished for its invigorating properties. The ancient Egyptians used it for its digestive and mood-lifting effects, while Roman soldiers are said to have worn crowns of peppermint to inspire their courage and sharpen their minds before battle. Modern research supports peppermint's ability to enhance cognitive function and alertness.

BAY LAUREL

was sacred to the ancient Greeks and Romans, who associated it with Apollo, the god of prophecy and wisdom. Oracles would chew bay leaves or burn them to induce a trance-like state, allowing them to access higher knowledge and inspiration.

CALMING AND GROUNDING

Herbs and spices have also played a crucial role in calming the spirit and grounding emotions. These include:

LAVENDER

is perhaps the most universally recognized herb for its calming effects. Ancient Romans used lavender in their baths to relax and soothe the body, while medieval monks would use it to calm their minds during prayer. Today, lavender oil is commonly used to alleviate anxiety, improve sleep, and create a sense of peace.

CHAMOMILE

has a long history of use as a calming agent. The Egyptians dedicated chamomile to the sun god Ra, believing it could cure fevers and calm the nerves. In European folk medicine, chamomile was used to treat sleeplessness and anxiety, and its gentle nature makes it a popular remedy still today.

FRANKINCENSE

has been used for millennia in religious and spiritual rituals. Ancient Egyptians burned frankincense in their temples as an offering to the gods, and it was used in embalming rituals to calm the spirit and purify the body. In the modern era, frankincense oil is valued for its ability to promote deep breathing and a meditative state, making it a staple in mindfulness practices.

REJUVENATION AND HEALING

Many herbs and spices have been revered for their ability to rejuvenate the body and spirit, aiding in recovery and restoring vitality:

EUCALYPTUS

has been used for centuries by Indigenous Australians, who valued it for its powerful healing properties, particularly for respiratory issues. The oil from eucalyptus leaves is still widely used today in steam inhalations and chest rubs to clear the airways and invigorate the body.

SAGE

has been a symbol of wisdom and longevity since ancient times. The Greeks and Romans believed sage could cure many ailments, and it was often associated with immortality. In various Indigenous cultures, sage is burned in smudging ceremonies to purify spaces and bodies, releasing negative energies and promoting spiritual healing.

GINGER

has been used in traditional Chinese and Ayurvedic medicine for over 2,500 years to stimulate the body's energy and support digestion. In ancient India, ginger was considered a universal medicine, used to treat ailments ranging from digestive issues to joint pain. Ginger oil is now recognized for its warming and invigorating effects, often used in massage therapy to soothe sore muscles and boost circulatin.

SPIRITUAL CONNECTION AND PROTECTION

Herbs and spices have also been used to protect and connect with the spiritual realm, providing a sense of safety and spiritual insight:

MYRRH

was highly valued in ancient Egypt and used in religious ceremonies and embalming. It was believed to connect the living with the divine. Myrrh oil was used to anoint the bodies of kings and priests. Today, myrrh is still used in spiritual practices for grounding and protection.

JUNIPER

has been used since ancient times for protection and purification. The ancient Greeks believed that burning juniper would ward off evil spirits, and it was often used in rituals to cleanse and sanctify. Juniper oil continues to be used in modern aromatherapy to purify the air, support spiritual clarity, and protect against negativity.

YARROW

was used by the ancient Druids as a protective herb, particularly in rituals that required courage and resilience. In Chinese medicine, yarrow has been used for centuries to balance the body's energy and support the immune system. Yarrow oil is now often used in blends to promote emotional healing and spiritual protection.

DAILY RITUALS FOR BALANCE AND CLARITY

Incorporating herbs and spices into your daily rituals can provide a sense of balance, grounding, and clarity, no matter what your day holds. Here are a few simple ways to weave these practices into your routine:

MORNING MINDFULNESS WITH ESSENTIAL OILS:

Start your day with a moment of mindfulness, setting the tone for what's to come. Diffuse rosemary or peppermint essential oil in your space as you sip your morning tea or coffee. These oils can help clear mental fog, energize your mind, and prepare you for the day ahead. If you're short on time, a drop or two of oil on a tissue or the palms of your hands can be inhaled deeply for a quick mental boost.

HERBAL TEAS FOR FOCUS AND CALM:

Swap out your regular cup of coffee for a calming or energizing herbal tea. Brew a pot of peppermint or ginger tea in the morning for an invigorating start, or choose lavender or chamomile in the evening to wind down. These teas not only offer the benefits of the herbs themselves but also encourage a moment of pause in your day—a time to sit, sip, and reflect.

SAGE AND SWEETGRASS FOR DAILY CLEARING:

As you transition between activities—whether moving from work to home life or winding down at the end of the day—use sage or sweetgrass to clear your space. Light a small bundle and allow the smoke to purify your surroundings, letting go of any lingering stress or negativity. This simple practice can help create calm and sacredness in your everyday life.

MODERN APPLICATIONS FOR HEALING AND REJUVENATION

Herbs and oils can also play a crucial role in your self-care routine, helping to rejuvenate your body and mind:

HEALING BATHS WITH EPSOM SALTS AND OILS:
After a long day, draw a bath and add a handful of Epsom salts along with a few drops of essential oils like eucalyptus or lavender. The salts help soothe sore muscles and detoxify, while the oils promote relaxation and healing. This ritual not only rejuvenates your body but also provides a quiet space for reflection and self-care.

DIY SKINCARE WITH NATURAL INGREDIENTS:
Create simple skincare products using the power of herbs and oils. For example, you can make a calming face mist by steeping dried lavender in hot water, then straining and adding a few drops of chamomile essential oil. Store it in a spray bottle and use it throughout the day to refresh your skin and calm your mind. Or, try mixing coconut oil with a few drops of frankincense or rose oil for a nourishing face or body moisturizer.

AROMATHERAPY FOR RESTORATIVE SLEEP:
Struggling with sleep is a common challenge in our modern world. Use oils like lavender, chamomile, or frankincense in a diffuser by your bedside to create a peaceful atmosphere conducive to sleep. You can also make a simple pillow spray with water and a few drops of these oils to help you drift off to a restful night's sleep.

RITUALS FOR SPIRITUAL CONNECTION AND INTENTION

Herbs and spices have a unique ability to deepen your spiritual practices, helping you set intentions and connect with your inner self:

INTENTIONAL JOURNALING WITH HERB-INFUSED INK:

Add a unique touch to your journaling practice by infusing your ink with herbs. You can create an ink infusion by simmering herbs like rosemary, sage, or mint in water, then straining and mixing the liquid with a natural ink base. As you write, the scent of the herbs will remind you of the intentions you're setting, making your journaling practice both a sensory and spiritual experience.

MOON RITUALS AND CRYSTALS:

Use the phases of the moon as a guide for setting intentions and releasing what no longer serves you. During the new moon, cleanse your space with sage or palo santo, and set new intentions with the help of crystals like moonstone or amethyst. On the full moon, use oils like sandalwood or myrrh to anoint your altar and release old energies, embracing the cycle of renewal and growth.

BRING IT ALL TOGETHER

Incorporating these practices into your modern life doesn't require a complete overhaul of your daily routine. Start with small, intentional steps—adding a few drops of essential oil to your bath, brewing a cup of herbal tea, or lighting a stick of incense during your meditation. Over time, these simple acts will create a deeper connection to the natural world and your inner wisdom.

As you continue your wisdom and wonder journey, remember that these herbs and oils are tools—ancient allies that can support you in crafting a life of balance, clarity, and intention. Whether you're seeking inspiration, calm, rejuvenation, or spiritual connection, integrating these practices into your daily life will help you navigate this next chapter with grace and empowerment.

THE TRANSFORMATIVE POWER OF MUSIC

Music is more than just sound—it's a language that speaks directly to the soul. Throughout history, music has played a central role in rituals, celebrations, and personal reflection. Its ability to soothe, inspire, motivate, and create sacred spaces makes it an invaluable companion as you meet your third chapter with intention and wisdom.

SOOTHING THE MIND AND SPIRIT

In the whirlwind of modern life, finding moments of peace can be a challenge. Music offers a direct pathway to tranquility, helping to calm the mind and soothe the spirit:

RELAXATION AND MEDITATION:
Soft, instrumental music or nature sounds can create a serene environment for meditation and relaxation. Whether it's the gentle flow of a harp, the distant echo of a flute, or the rhythmic sounds of ocean waves, these melodies help quiet the mind, allowing you to sink into a state of deep calm. Incorporating such music into your evening routine can signal to your body that it's time to unwind, promoting restful sleep and a sense of well-being.

HEALING FREQUENCIES:
Certain types of music are designed to resonate with specific frequencies that are believed to promote healing and balance. For example, music tuned to 432 Hz is said to have a calming effect, aligning with the natural vibrations of the earth. Similarly, binaural beats—tones that use two slightly different frequencies in each ear—can induce states of relaxation, focus, or deep meditation, depending on the frequencies used.

INSPIRING CREATIVITY AND REFLECTION

Music has the unique ability to inspire creativity and foster deep reflection, making it an ideal companion for journaling, art, or simply contemplating life's journey:

CLASSICAL AND AMBIENT MUSIC FOR FOCUS:
Classical music has long been associated with intellectual and creative pursuits. Composers like Bach, Beethoven, Mozart, or Debussy can provide a rich auditory backdrop that enhances focus and encourages thoughtful reflection. Ambient music, with its soothing and often repetitive structures, can also help create a mental space where ideas flow freely and creative expression is nurtured.

WORLD MUSIC FOR CULTURAL CONNECTION:
Exploring music from different cultures can broaden your perspective and connect you to the diverse expressions of the human experience. Whether it's the haunting sounds of a Native American flute, the rhythmic beats of African drumming, or the melodic chants of Indian ragas, world music can inspire a sense of global connectedness and deepen your appreciation for the many ways people celebrate and reflect through music.

MOTIVATING ACTION AND ENERGY

There are times in your journey when you may need a boost of energy or motivation to take on new challenges or push through periods of doubt. Music can be the spark that ignites your inner fire:

UPLIFTING RHYTHMS FOR PHYSICAL MOVEMENT:
Energetic music with strong rhythms can be a powerful motivator for physical activity, whether it's a morning walk, a yoga session, or a dance break. Fast-paced genres like Afrobeat, Latin dance, or pop can elevate your mood, increase your stamina, and encourage you to move with joy and enthusiasm. The physicality of movement, paired with uplifting music, reinforces a positive connection between mind and body.

ANTHEMS OF EMPOWERMENT:
Sometimes, you need a soundtrack that reminds you of your strength and potential. Songs with empowering lyrics and bold melodies can serve as anthems of resilience and self-confidence. Whether it's the soulful voice of Aretha Franklin, the revolutionary spirit of Nina Simone, or the contemporary empowerment of Beyoncé, these musical icons offer messages of strength and self-assurance that resonate deeply during moments of challenge and triumph.

CREATE SACRED SPACES AND RITUALS

Music has an almost magical ability to transform a space, making it sacred and inviting a deeper connection to the spiritual:

CHANTS AND MANTRAS FOR RITUALS:
The repetition of chants or mantras has been used in spiritual practices across the world to focus the mind and open the heart. Gregorian chants, Hindu mantras, or Buddhist chanting can create a sacred atmosphere in your space, helping you center yourself during rituals or meditation. The rhythmic repetition of these sounds can induce a meditative state, making it easier to connect with your inner self and the divine.

MUSIC FOR CEREMONIAL MOMENTS:
When marking significant moments in your wisdom and wonder journey—such as the final Turn, which may culminate in a ceremony—music can enhance the sense of sacredness and celebration. Choose music that resonates with the emotions you wish to invoke, whether it's the deep reverence of a Native American drum circle, the joyful celebration of a Celtic jig, or the serene beauty of a string quartet. These sounds can elevate the moment, making it both meaningful and memorable.

CURATING A PERSONAL PLAYLIST:
One of the simplest yet most effective ways to incorporate music into your journey is by curating a personal playlist. This could be a collection of songs that speak to different aspects of your path—songs that soothe you, inspire creativity, energize your spirit, or help you create a sacred space. As you move through the twelve Turns, your playlist can evolve, reflecting your growth and the unique phases of your journey. I have created a Spotify playlist called WonderCrone #1 that features 100 songs about women, by women. The music ranges widely in genre and tone, which reflects the diversity of life experiences we bring as we age. Check it out and enjoy!

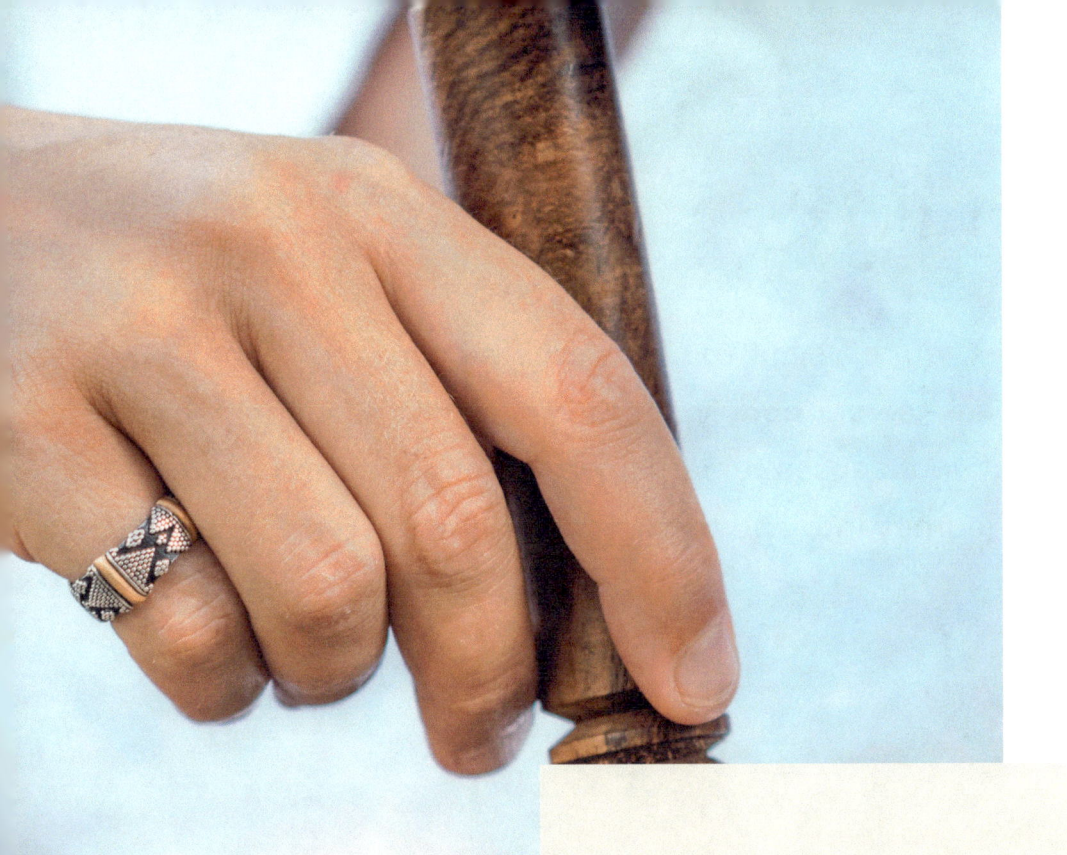

BRING IT ALL TOGETHER

Music is a powerful ally in your wisdom and wonder journey, offering a direct line to the emotions, energies, and spiritual insights that define this transformative time. By intentionally choosing music that resonates with your needs—whether for soothing, inspiring, motivating, or creating sacred spaces—you can enhance your connection to yourself and the world around you. As you explore the Turns of this workbook, allow music to guide you, to accompany your reflections, and to celebrate your milestones. Let it be the soundtrack of your entry and a constant companion that supports you in writing this next chapter of your life with wisdom, grace, and joy.

THE STAGE IS SET

Now the stage is set for you to begin! You have created a sacred space that includes items that speak to your body, mind, and soul. You have created a space that invites all of your senses to participate in reflection and contemplation as you journey into and through your third chapter.

Bon voyage!

> Ruminate. Decide. Then change your mind. Decide again. There is no hurry and there are no right or wrong answers to any of this.

turn 1

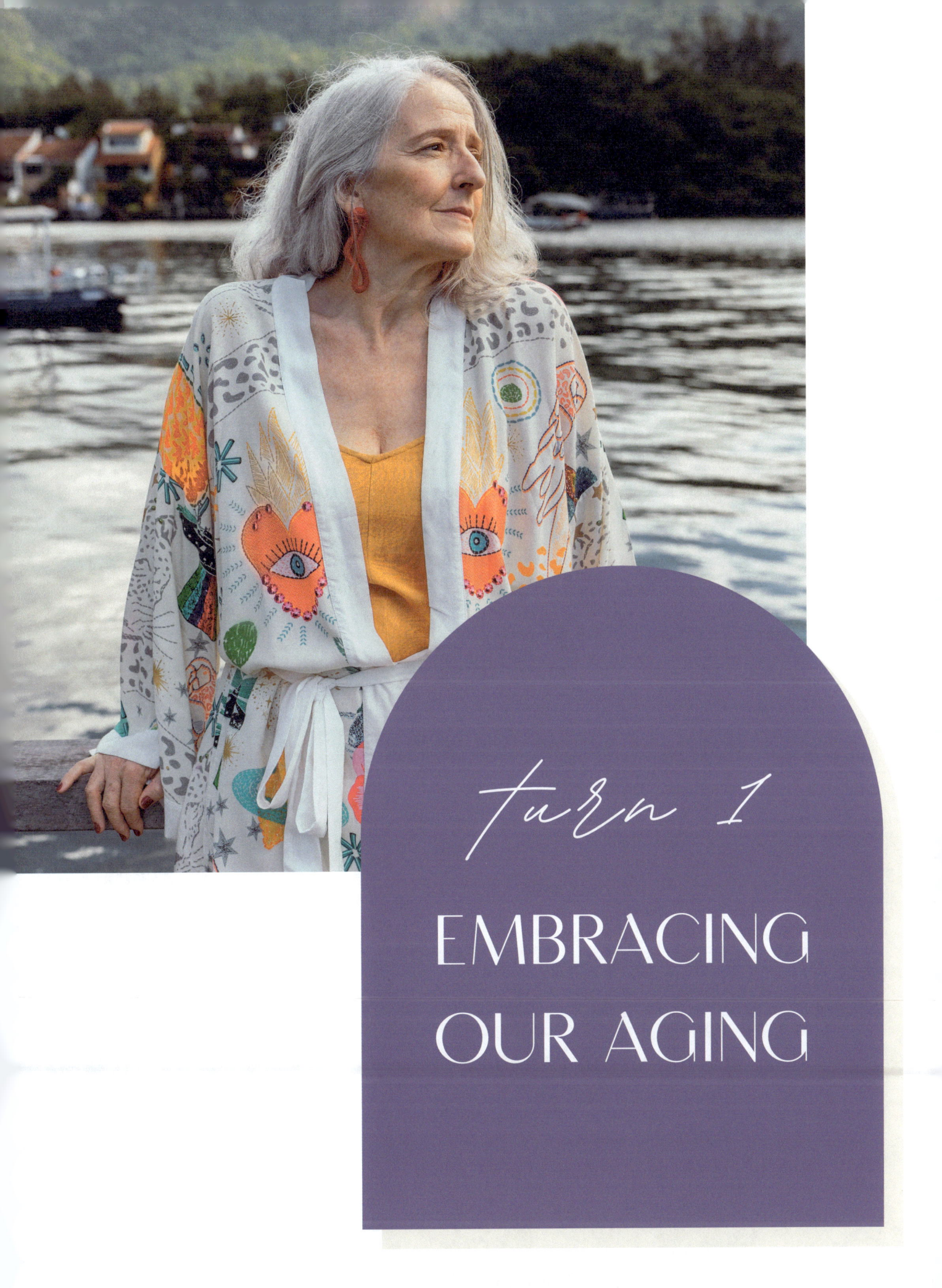

EMBRACING OUR AGING

Aging is a curious thing. It sneaks up on us, subtly at first—a new line here, a gray hair there—until one day we find ourselves staring in the mirror, recognizing the face but knowing it's transformed by time. In a society that worships youth, the transition into older age can feel like stepping into a foreign land. We're conditioned to see age as a decline or diminishment, something to resist rather than embrace.

How do we refer to ourselves as we age? Senior? Old lady? Me, I like crone. To be honest—crone hasn't exactly enjoyed the best PR. Western dictionaries tend to paint the crone as a haggard, cruel, withered old woman. Not exactly the kind of image you want on your vision board. But here's the thing—language evolves, and so do we. Think of how the words Gay, Black, Queer, or even Impressionist were derogatory terms. The thing is, each of these groups turned around and owned these labels, making them identity statements of power.

While some may still cling to that outdated stereotype, to me, the crone of today is a woman of power, wisdom, and grace. She is the embodiment of a life well-lived, a life rich with experiences that have polished her into a gem of insight and strength. But why stop at reclaiming crone as a term of respect? Let's dig deeper into its roots.

The word crone shares linguistic ties with crown—a symbol of sovereignty, authority, and dignity. And from the Greek Cronus, the god of time, we find a connection to the idea of the crone as a keeper of time's secrets, a woman who has journeyed through the seasons of life and emerged with a unique understanding of the world.

> The crone is a woman who is no longer shaped or controlled by the judgment from others.

Nevertheless, many women are not prepared to claim this title. For this reason, we will continue to anchor this workbook on wisdom and wonder, on cultivating our third chapter. We are talking about the same thing: finding new purpose, continuous evolution, transformation! It's about taking the raw material of our experiences and refining it into the wisdom that will guide us through the rest of our life's journey. We take a fresh perspective on aging—one that is rooted in self-respect, self-knowledge, and a deep sense of purpose.

So, as you step into this Turn, I invite you to see this time not as an ending, but as a beginning. The beginning of a time when you are freer than ever to be yourself, to express the fullness of who you are, and to share the depth of your wisdom with the world. You are not just growing older; you are stepping into your power.

EXERCISES TO EMBRACE OUR AGING

How do you refer to others in your age group? Or to yourself? Middle age is behind us. What comes next?

How would you respond if someone called you a crone? Do you flinch, or do you respond with pride and confidence?

In the coming days and weeks, test the word you are most comfortable with friends and family and see what their reaction is. Perhaps even introduce them to the powerful connotations of the crone and identify those who will support – and even embrace – this journey you've begun.

INTENTION

All life unfolds in stages, each phase in its turn. I love the wisdom that life has brought me. I am inspired as I explore and craft the autumn of my life. I welcome the elder I am.

Your intention for Turn #1:

NOTES

turn 2

ACCEPTING THE FULL CYCLE OF LIFE

What could be more natural than to ripen, mature, and age? Just as the seasons shift and the sun sets each day, aging is a fundamental part of life's rhythm. Yet, in our culture, there's an underlying fear of aging—a fear that is often less about the process itself and more about what we've been taught to associate with it. Are we truly afraid of growing old, or have we simply been conditioned to fear what old age represents in a society that glorifies youth?

There's a powerful proverb in Africa: "Every time an elder dies, a library is lost." This saying reminds us that elders are the keepers of wisdom, their lives rich with experiences and lessons that, when shared, enrich the lives of those who come after them. In our modern, commercialized world, where youth and power are often idolized, the wisdom of age can be overlooked or undervalued. Yet, it is this wisdom, especially the wisdom of women, that has long held the fabric of families and communities together. Women are the bridges between what was and what could be, the ones who carry forward the stories, the traditions, and the hard-earned truths.

We, the women stepping into our third chapters, have already weathered so much. We've survived the turbulence of youth, the intensity of our child-bearing years—whether we bore children or not—and the challenges of balancing our roles in family, work, and society. Now, we find ourselves standing on new ground, looking into the mirror and seeing reflections of our mothers, grandmothers, and the many women who came before us. Our bodies, once so firm and resilient, have changed. We ache in places that once felt invincible, and our bodies react to food, drink, and life itself in ways that are new and sometimes unwelcome. We face illness, both in ourselves and in those we care about. And, perhaps most strikingly, we often find that we are now the oldest in the room.

> Aging, like anything new, can be intimidating. But it is also a natural, inevitable part of life. To discuss aging openly is to demystify the process, to strip away the fear, and embrace the truth that aging is as natural as the changing of the seasons. As we build networks and communities of elder women, we learn from each other—sharing our gifts, our fears, our insights, and our joys. Together, we reclaim the power of aging, transforming it from something to be feared into something to be celebrated.

> **Women are bridges from what once was to what may yet be.**

In her insightful book Crones Don't Whine: Concentrated Wisdom for Juicy Women, Dr. Jean Shinoda Bolen highlights the unique power of the sister, mother, and crone archetypes in women, allowing us to identify with each other across national, racial, and religious boundaries. This third phase of life invites us to reflect on the meaning of life, and more specifically, the meaning of our own lives. What legacy will we leave? What wisdom will we share? In accepting the full cycle of life, we honor the journey that has brought us here, and we step forward into our cronehood with grace and intention.

EXERCISES: EXPLORING THE FULL CYCLE

REFLECT ON YOUR JOURNEY:

Consider the life stages you've already passed through—childhood, adolescence, adulthood. What did you learn in each stage? How did each prepare you for where you are now? Take some time to write down your thoughts, focusing on the wisdom you've gained and how it can guide you through this next phase.

EMBRACE THE CHANGES:

Think about the physical, emotional, and spiritual changes you've noticed as you've aged. How have these changes impacted your view of yourself? How can you embrace these changes rather than resist them? Write down one or two positive aspects of aging that you want to focus on moving forward.

BUILD YOUR WISDOM AND WONDER COMMUNITY:

Reach out to other women in your life who are also entering or are already in their crone years. Start a conversation about aging—what fears or hopes do they have? What wisdom have they gained? Consider forming a small group that meets regularly to discuss your journeys, share insights, and support one another.

INTENTION

I accept the full cycle of life, knowing that each stage brings its own wisdom and beauty. As I enter this new phase, I do so with an open heart, embracing the changes and challenges that come with it.

Your Intention for Turn #2:

NOTES

turn 3

LIVING MINDFULLY

In the West, we're often conditioned to equate busyness with success. From a young age, we're taught to juggle multiple roles—housekeeper, career woman, mother, partner, bestie—while squeezing in a little "self-care" if time allows. We rush from one task to the next, our minds always spinning with what-ifs, should-haves, and what's-next. It's no wonder that many of us rarely feel truly present in our bodies or our lives.

But then, life shifts. Children grow up and carve out their own life paths. We retire from careers that once defined us. Our homes—once bustling centers of activity—quiet down, and even our relationships may no longer fit the people we've become. Suddenly, the pace slows, and the roles that once filled our days begin to fade. In a society that idolizes youth, we may feel as though we've lost our bearings, unsure of where we fit in this new phase of life.

> Moving into our third chapter, we can recalibrate how we live in the world.

Yet, this transition into our third chapter offers a powerful opportunity to redefine how we walk through the world. Unlike the frantic pace of our earlier years, this phase invites us to slow down, to be more intentional, and to embrace a different way of living—one that is mindful, aware, and gentle. It's a shift from doing to being, from constant motion to conscious presence.

Other cultures have long understood the value of mindfulness—a way of living that is rooted in the present moment, free from the endless cycle of worry and regret. Be Here Now may sound simple, but it's a discipline that requires practice, patience, and a deep commitment to self-compassion. It means setting boundaries, honoring our own needs, and living consciously rather than on autopilot.

As we move into the wisdom and wonder of our third chapter, we are gifted with the time and space to recalibrate. We no longer need to be everything to everyone—a role we were never truly able to fulfill anyway. Instead, we can focus on being fully present for ourselves, cultivating a life that aligns with our values and desires. This is the gift of cronehood: the freedom to live mindfully, with intention and grace, in a way that honors the wisdom we've gathered along the way.

EXERCISES: CULTIVATING MINDFULNESS

MINDFUL BREATHING:

Begin each day with a few minutes of mindful breathing. Sit quietly and focus on your breath as it moves in and out. Notice the sensations in your body, the rise and fall of your chest, and the air as it fills your lungs. If your mind wanders, gently bring it back to your breath. This simple practice can help ground you in the present moment and set a mindful tone for the day.

CREATE A DAILY RITUAL:

Choose a daily activity—such as drinking your morning tea, taking a walk, or tending to a garden—and turn it into a mindfulness practice. Focus entirely on the activity, noticing each detail, each movement, and each sensation. Allow yourself to be fully immersed in the moment, free from distractions or multitasking.

SET BOUNDARIES:

Reflect on the areas of your life where you feel overstretched or overwhelmed. Where can you set boundaries to protect your time and energy? Write down one or two boundaries you'd like to establish and make a commitment to honor them. This is a key step in living mindfully—knowing your limits and respecting them.

INTENTION

I choose to live mindfully, embracing each moment with awareness and presence. I honor my needs, set healthy boundaries, and cultivate a life of intentional, conscious living. I align myself with the world around me with gratitude and appreciation.

Your Intention for Turn #3:

NOTES

turn 4

RESPECTING COMPASSIONATELY

There are moments in life when it feels like the world is pulling us in too many directions, stretching our patience and compassion to the breaking point. When we're under pressure, it's easy to lash out—anger, hasty words, or biting sarcasm slipping from our lips before we even realize it. But it's precisely in these moments, when we feel most tested, that patience and compassion can have the most profound healing effect.

Being stretched thin can take many forms. In Turn #3, we explored ways to live more mindfully each day. Now, think back to that exploration. Where did you feel life was too chaotic, knocking you off balance and out of mindful living? In those moments, how did you relate to those around you—or to yourself? Likely, it wasn't with the compassion or respect that you truly deserve.

We may think we're listening to our friends, family, or colleagues, but are we? Compassionate listening is very different from the default mode many of us fall into—listening to fix, correct, or advise. True compassionate listening is about creating a safe space for the other person to express themselves without fear of judgment or unsolicited advice. It's about being fully present, offering your ear, and your heart, without trying to fix what's wrong.

The basic principles of compassionate listening are simple but transformative:

1. **Don't try to fix the problem or give advice unless specifically asked.** Sometimes, the most healing thing you can do is simply to listen.

2. **Embrace silence and patience.** Allowing space for someone to speak at their own pace can help them find their voice and express their true feelings.

3. **Don't take what is said personally.** Compassionate listening requires us to set aside our own ego and focus entirely on the speaker.

4. **Avoid getting defensive or feeling attacked.** When something concerning is said, try to remain open and receptive rather than defensive.

5. **Reflect what is said rather than commenting on it.** Simple reflections like, "I hear that this is a difficult time for you," can show that you are truly listening.

6. **Offer a sympathetic ear, but never pity.** Pity can feel patronizing, while genuine empathy empowers the other person.

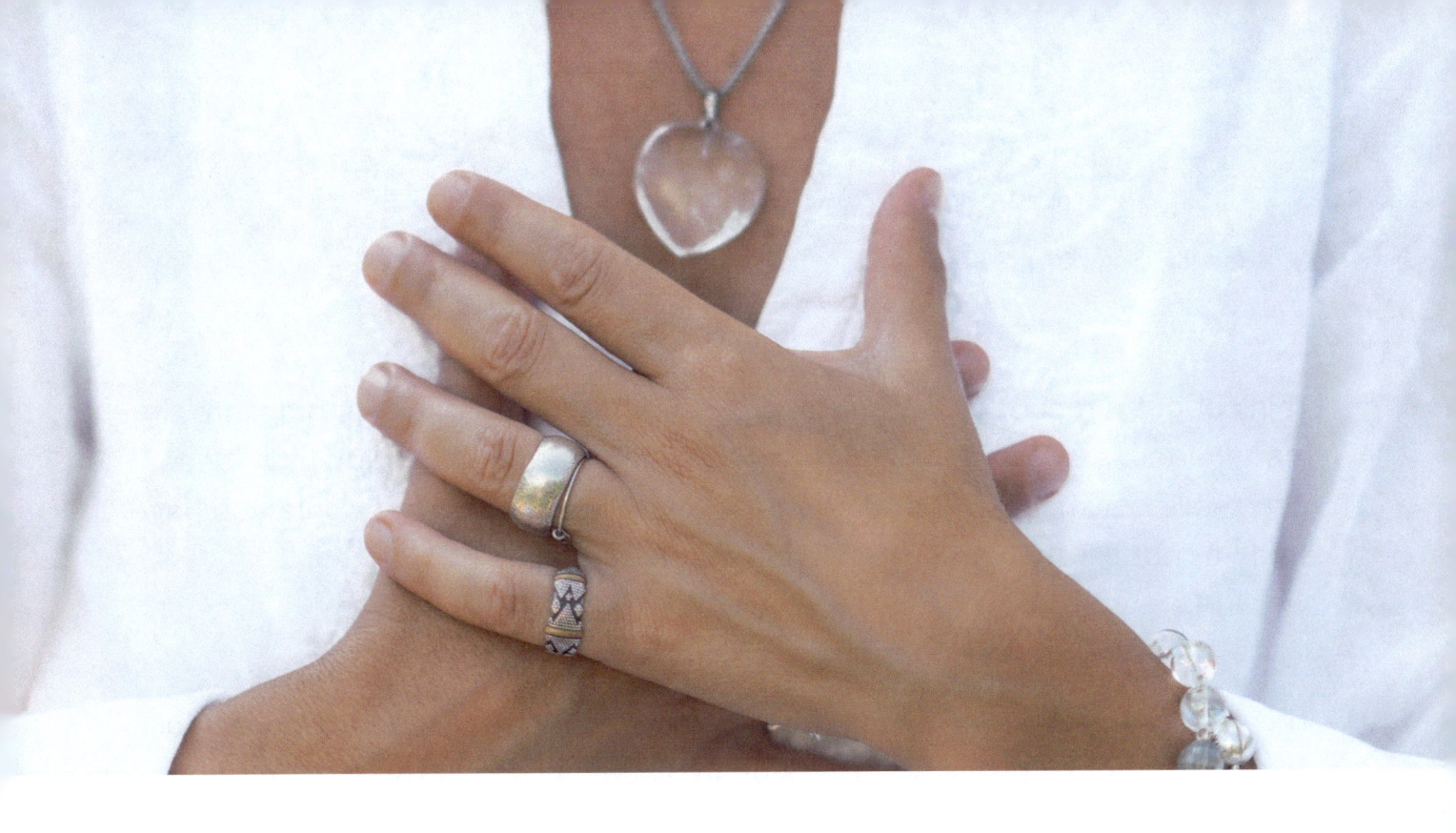

This practice of compassion doesn't stop with how we listen to others—it's just as crucial in our internal dialogue. Many of us have an inner critic who's been a constant companion, whispering in our ears about all the ways we've fallen short. The voice of the inner critic can be harsh, relentless, and far less forgiving than we would ever be with others.

Part of aging with wisdom and wonder is learning to resolve—not simply ignore—that inner critic. It's about retraining our internal conversation to be as kind, compassionate, and loving as we strive to be with others. After all, if we can offer understanding and patience to a friend, why not extend the same grace to ourselves? We deserve it.

> Offer a sympathetic ear, but never with pity.

EXERCISES: CULTIVATING COMPASSIONATE LISTENING

REFLECT ON A RECENT CONVERSATION:
Think about a recent conversation where you found yourself slipping into the mode of fixing, advising, or judging. How might that conversation have been different if you had practiced compassionate listening? What could you have said—or not said—to create a more supportive space?

PRACTICE COMPASSIONATE LISTENING:
The next time someone comes to you with a problem or concern, consciously practice the principles of compassionate listening. Resist the urge to offer advice unless asked, and focus on reflecting their feelings back to them. Notice how this approach affects the conversation and the connection between you.

REFRAME YOUR INNER DIALOGUE:
Spend some time reflecting on the ways you speak to yourself, especially in moments of stress or self-doubt. Write down a few of the harshest things your inner critic tends to say. Then, take a moment to reframe these statements with compassion and kindness, as you would if you were speaking to a dear friend.

INTENTION

I choose to listen with compassion, both to others and to myself. I create space for healing and understanding, knowing that true connection begins with an open heart and a gentle ear.

Your Intention for Turn #4:

NOTES

turn 5

HONORING SELF

How often do we truly take the time to be good to ourselves? In a world that often demands so much from us, the idea of honoring oneself can sometimes get lost in the shuffle. But self-honoring isn't about over-indulging or pampering in excess—it's about nourishing ourselves in ways that support our well-being, body, mind, and spirit.

Honoring oneself means choosing good, healthy food that fuels our bodies, seeking fresh air and clean water that revitalizes us, surrounding ourselves with beauty and calm, and engaging in joyful activities that feed our souls. When we take the time to honor ourselves, we create positive feedback loops within our bodies, triggering the release of "happy hormones" that enhance our mood and overall health.

> Honor yourself by taking stock.

These "happy hormones" include dopamine, serotonin, oxytocin, and endorphins—each playing a unique role in our well-being:

- **Dopamine** is the hormone associated with pleasure, learning, and memory—crucial elements that we should continue to nurture as we age. Engaging in activities that challenge our minds and bring us joy can stimulate dopamine, helping us stay mentally sharp and emotionally fulfilled.

- **Serotonin** is the regulator of mood, sleep, appetite, and digestion. It also plays a vital role in learning and memory, making it essential for maintaining a balanced and peaceful life. Activities that bring a sense of peace and contentment, like spending time in nature or practicing mindfulness, can boost serotonin levels.

- **Oxytocin** is often called the "love hormone," as it increases with physical affection and fosters feelings of trust, empathy, and bonding. Nurturing relationships and practicing kindness—both to ourselves and others—can elevate oxytocin, deepening our connections and enhancing our sense of belonging.

- **Endorphins** are the body's natural painkillers, released during reward-producing activities, whether they're healthy or unhealthy. This makes them a double-edged sword. Choosing activities that promote well-being, like exercise or creative expression, ensures that our endorphin rushes come from positive sources.

What nourished us in our younger years may not serve us in the same way as we enter our third chapter. Yet, we often continue with habits and activities simply because "we've always done that." Honoring oneself as a crone means taking stock—observing how we spend our time and identifying which activities truly bring us joy and satisfaction.

This doesn't mean we need to sort out all our behaviors in one go. Start small. Notice the activities that uplift you, that make you feel vibrant and alive. Gradually, build on these nurturing practices, creating a life that honors who you are today and supports who you are becoming.

EXERCISES: HONORING YOUR EMERGING SELF

INVENTORY OF JOY:
Spend some time reflecting on the activities and habits that currently fill your days. Which ones bring you true joy and satisfaction? Which ones feel like obligations or outdated routines? Make a list of activities that you want to keep, and consider one or two that you'd like to release or replace with something more nourishing.

CREATE A SELF-HONORING RITUAL:
Choose one small, nurturing activity that you can commit to doing daily. It might be as simple as a morning stretch, a short walk in the fresh air, or a few minutes of quiet reflection with a cup of tea. Let this activity be a daily reminder of your commitment to honoring yourself and your well-being.

TUNE INTO YOUR HAPPY HORMONES:
Over the next week, pay attention to how your body feels during different activities. Notice when you feel a sense of pleasure, peace, connection, or energy. Write down the activities that seem to trigger positive feelings and consider how you can incorporate more of them into your life.

INTENTION

I honor myself by choosing activities and habits that nourish my body, mind, and spirit. I am committed to creating a life that supports my well-being and celebrates who I am as I age with wisdom and wonder.

Your intention for Turn #5:

NOTES

turn 6

LOVING SELF

Our earliest lessons in love come from our families and those who surrounded us when we were very young. For some, these lessons were nurturing, providing a foundation of security and self-worth. But for others, the lessons were far less kind, leaving wounds that can take a lifetime to heal. If this resonates with you, I want you to know, deep in your heart and on a cellular level: You did not choose the family you were born into. You did nothing to deserve any physical or emotional abuse you may have suffered as a child. As we age consciously, lovingly, and fully, there is much to unlearn and relearn.

Whether or not we can only love others as much as we love ourselves, the truth is that loving ourselves is essential to living our best lives. This is true at any age, but the journey of intentional, powerful aging offers a unique opportunity to examine what self-love truly looks, sounds, and feels like.

Self-love is not about self-indulgence. It's not about placating an unruly inner child or treating yourself as an afterthought. Self-love is about embracing the whole of who you are—your strengths and your limitations, your triumphs and your challenges. Appreciating all that you bring to life and living, having compassion for your down days and shortfalls, and setting healthy boundaries to protect your energy and well-being is self-love. Also, maintain a sense of humor to carry you through both the good and not-so-good days.

> When we love ourselves, we live our best lives.

Some of us might excel in certain dimensions of self-love while struggling in others. And that's okay. The fullness of self-love can ebb and flow, depending on what's happening in your life. The goal isn't to achieve some strict, superior uniformity in how you love yourself. The goal is to understand how your self-love looks today and consider how you might deepen, strengthen, or cultivate greater self-love over time.

As we explored in Turn #5, positive behaviors release those wonderful "happy hormones" that uplift our mood and enhance our well-being. Loving oneself is healing—mentally, physically, and spiritually. It's the foundation of a life well-lived and the cornerstone of your journey into your third chapter.

EXERCISES: EXPLORING THE FULL CYCLE

REFLECT ON YOUR SELF-LOVE JOURNEY:
Spend some time reflecting on your relationship with self-love throughout your life. How have your feelings toward yourself evolved? What areas of self-love do you feel strongest in, and where do you feel there's room for growth? Write down your reflections as a way to gain insight into your current self-love landscape.

PRACTICE SELF-COMPASSION:
Choose one area of your life where you tend to be hard on yourself—whether it's a perceived shortcoming, a past mistake, or an ongoing challenge. Take a moment to practice self-compassion in this area. What would you say to a dear friend going through the same thing? Now, say those words to yourself. Allow yourself to feel the warmth of your own kindness.

CREATE A SELF-LOVE RITUAL:
Develop a small daily or weekly ritual that honors your commitment to self-love. This could be as simple as looking in the mirror each morning and offering yourself a kind word, or taking a few minutes each evening to reflect on something you appreciate about yourself. You might review the section earlier in this workbook about herbs and spices to see ways to add these to a self-love ritual. Let this ritual be a reminder that you are deserving of love, respect, and care—especially from yourself.

INTENTION

I choose to love myself fully, embracing all I am with compassion, appreciation, and humor. I honor the journey of self-love as a vital part of my aging, nurturing myself with the care and respect I deserve.

Your Intention for Turn #6:

NOTES

turn 7

APPRECIATING SIMPLICITY

As we enter our third chapter, many of us feel a natural urge to simplify our lives. The lifestyle changes that often accompany this phase—whether by choice or circumstance—foster a desire to downsize, live lighter, and feel less encumbered by the material possessions we've accumulated over the years. Simplifying our lives and appreciating simplicity allows us to focus on what is most essential, stripping away the excess to reveal the core of what truly matters.

There are countless ways to simplify, but one of the most obvious starting points is decluttering and downsizing. The benefits of these actions are manifold—more time, better finances, less stress, and a greater ability to live fully in the present moment. Letting go of once-loved but no longer-needed possessions can be liberating, offering a sense of lightness and freedom. And what better way to pass on these items than to donate them to those who can make use of them? Consider giving professional clothes to college graduates, women who were previously incarcerated, or those seeking to restart their lives. There's likely an organization or group near you that would welcome these contributions.

Create a foundation of greater clarity, connection, and direction.

But simplicity goes beyond just material possessions. It extends to how we spend our time, the goals we set for ourselves, and the way we connect with others. Are our lives filled with rushed schedules and relentless deadlines, or do we move at a pace that's more in tune with the rhythms of nature? Do we maintain a large circle of acquaintances, or do we cherish a few close friendships that nourish our souls? Do we fill our calendars with complicated events, or do we find joy in simple gatherings with loved ones—sharing a meal, walking in nature, or engaging in meaningful conversation?

Appreciating simplicity is about returning to what is most important, stripping away the noise and clutter that can obscure our clarity, connection, and direction. As we age in wisdom and wonder, we have the opportunity to create a foundation built on simplicity— one that supports greater peace, presence, and purpose in our lives.

EXERCISES: CULTIVATING SIMPLICITY

DECLUTTER YOUR SPACE:

Choose one area of your home—perhaps a closet, a room, or even just a drawer—and spend some time decluttering. As you go through your belongings, ask yourself: Does this item still serve me? If not, consider letting it go. Donate items that are still in good condition to those who need them, and feel the lightness that comes from releasing what no longer serves you.

SIMPLIFY YOUR SCHEDULE:

Take a look at your calendar for the week. Are there activities or commitments that feel more like obligations than joys? Consider simplifying your schedule by saying no to events that don't align with your values or bring you fulfillment. Instead, make time for activities that bring you peace, whether it's spending time in nature, practicing mindfulness, or simply relaxing with a good book.

RECONNECT WITH NATURE:

Spend time outdoors, immersing yourself in the simplicity and beauty of the natural world. Whether it's a walk in the park, a hike in the woods, or simply sitting in your garden, allow yourself to tune into the pace of nature. Notice the sights, sounds, and smells around you, and let them guide you back to a simpler, more grounded way of being.

INTENTION

I choose to appreciate simplicity in all areas of my life, focusing on what truly matters. I let go of what no longer serves me, creating space for clarity, connection, and peace.

Your Intention for Turn #7:

NOTES

turn 8

LOVING GAIA

Remember that old commercial that warned, "It's not nice to fool Mother Nature!"? It turns out, that wasn't just a catchy tagline—it was a profound truth that we've collectively ignored for far too long. Over the past century, especially in the West, we've been fooling Mother Nature on a grand scale. We've over-used, over-exploited, over-produced, over-consumed, and over-trashed our planet, Gaia, pushing her to the brink. We are now nearing—and in some cases, crossing—planetary boundaries that are essential for sustaining life.

In many ways, the depletion of our planet mirrors the depletion we've experienced on a personal level. Just as we've drained Gaia's resources, we've often drained our energy, health, and well-being in the pursuit of more, more, more. And just as we must begin to heal ourselves, so too must we begin to heal the earth. Both processes are interconnected, and both must start now.

It's easy to feel overwhelmed by the scale of the global climate crisis. The problems seem so vast, so deeply entrenched, that it can feel like there's little one individual can do. And while it's true that no single person can fix the entire problem, each of us can make a difference. We must acknowledge that differences are related to culture, privilege, wealth, and resource use. Yet, we have guiding stars. Consider the pioneering work of Wangari Maathai, the first African woman to win a Nobel Peace Prize for her work on environmental conservation, representative democracy, and defending women's rights.

> The earth is our mother, the sky is our father, and everything in between is our brother and sisters.

Our consumer habits drive our economies, and by choosing to spend our money on sustainable foods, opting for less polluting modes of transportation, and stepping away from fast food, fast fashion, and other forms of consumption that harm the planet, we can begin to live more gently on Gaia.

First Nation peoples have long understood the importance of living in harmony with the earth. The Iroquois, for example, embrace the Seventh-Generation principle, which teaches that the earth is our mother, the sky is our father, and everything in between is our brothers and sisters. This principle reminds us that everyone and everything deserves respect and the right to be listened to. Before taking any action that affects nature, we should ask ourselves: How will this impact the next seven generations?

In the West, a growing movement echoes this wisdom through the seven Rs: Redesign, Reduce, Reuse, Repair, Renew, Recover, and Recycle. These principles offer us practical ways to minimize our footprint and contribute to the healing of our planet. By incorporating these practices into our daily lives, we honor Gaia and begin to restore the balance that has been lost.

EXERCISES: LIVING IN HARMONY WITH GAIA

EVALUATE YOUR FOOTPRINT:

Take some time to reflect on your current lifestyle and consumer habits. Where can you make changes that would reduce your impact on the planet? Consider areas like food, transportation, clothing, and household goods. Choose one or two small changes to implement this week, and notice how it feels to live more sustainably.

ADOPT THE SEVEN RS:

The next time someone comes to you with a problem or concern, consciously practice the principles of compassionate listening. Resist the urge to offer advice unless asked, and focus on reflecting their feelings back to them. Notice how this approach affects the conversation and the connection between you.

RECONNECT WITH NATURE:

Spend time outdoors, consciously reconnecting with the natural world. Whether it's a walk in the park, a hike in the woods, or simply sitting in your garden, allow yourself to feel the earth beneath your feet, breathe in the fresh air, and appreciate the beauty of Gaia. Reflect on the ways you can show love and respect for the earth in your daily life.

INTENTION

I choose to live in harmony with Gaia, honoring her by making sustainable choices and reducing my impact on the planet. I am committed to loving and protecting our earth for future generations.

Your Intention for Turn #8:

NOTES

turn 9

NAVIGATING BELIEFS

Aging in wisdom and wonder is inherently a process that challenges prevailing beliefs—especially our own. As we step into this new phase of life, we may find that our views, our voices, and even our very presence are met with resistance from others. Not everyone is going to appreciate the changes you're making or the direction your life is taking. This is why getting clarity on who you are in this final phase of life is essential. It's worth the time and effort (and the inevitable iterations) to understand and embrace your true self.

Remember, you are under no obligation to convince others about this process or where you are headed. Your journey is yours alone, and it is sacred. While it's natural to want others to understand and accept the choices you are making about your third chapter, your primary responsibility is to yourself—to live authentically and in alignment with your values and beliefs.

We are living in polarized, heated, and all-too-often mean-spirited times. Navigating beliefs in such an environment requires us to be mindful of the toxicity that can arise from engaging with ideas and positions that are out of alignment with our own. If we choose to rage against these forces, the stress hormones we discussed earlier will spike, likely causing more harm to our own bodies and minds than any impact on the opposing side. This isn't to advocate for passivity—action is necessary. But it's crucial to cultivate tools that allow us to move out of hostile situations, clear space for effective action, and maintain our well-being.

These tools might be as simple as counting slowly to ten and taking a deep breath, or using a phrase like, "We'll just have to agree to disagree." In some cases, it might involve firmly stating, "We have very different opinions, and I'm not going to engage with you on this." The key is to avoid adding more venom into the mix, as doing so rarely leads to anything positive or constructive.

> Honor your inner truth with clarity and resilience in the face of a polarized world.

Jean Shinoda Bolen, a groundbreaking Jungian psychologist and author of several foundational books on croning, offers wisdom for these challenging times. She notes that to have a life oriented to the Self—rather than one determined by persona, or how we are perceived by others—is a spiritual orientation. This means living a life that is guided by your inner truth and values, rather than external validation.

Bolen suggests that prayer can take many forms, within or beyond the bounds of established faith institutions. She describes prayer as a way to be touched by or in touch with divinity—a sacred moment that transcends daily thoughts and actions. For some, this might be dancing, chanting, grounding, gardening, creating art, cooking, writing, or engaging in any activity that supports your connection to the sacred.

Orienting your third chapter to the Self will help you navigate these difficult times with clarity, purpose, and resilience. It's about choosing to live in a way that honors your inner truth while cultivating the strength and tools needed to face the challenges of today's world.

EXERCISES: CLARIFYING AND PROTECTING YOUR BELIEFS

REFLECT ON YOUR CORE BELIEFS:

Spend some time reflecting on the beliefs that are most important to you at this stage of your life. What values guide your decisions and actions? How have your beliefs evolved over time? Write down your reflections to gain clarity on where you stand and what you hold most dear.

CREATE A TOOLKIT FOR NAVIGATING CONFLICT:

Identify a few phrases or actions that you can use when faced with conflict or hostility related to differing beliefs. Practice using these tools in low-stakes situations so that they become second nature when you need them most. This might include deep breathing, setting clear boundaries, or simply walking away from a heated discussion.

ENGAGE IN A SACRED PRACTICE:

Choose an activity that allows you to connect with your deeper self—whether it's meditation, prayer, dancing, or any other form of expression that feels sacred to you. Make this practice a regular part of your life, using it as a way to stay grounded and in touch with your true beliefs, even in the face of external challenges.

INTENTION

Choose an activity that allows you to connect with your deeper self—whether it's meditation, prayer, dancing, or any other form of expression that feels sacred to you. Make this practice a regular part of your life, using it as a way to stay grounded and in touch with your true beliefs, even in the face of external challenges.

Your intention for Turn #9:

NOTES

turn 10

SUSTAINING INTIMACY

In our culture, the concepts of desirability, intimacy, and sexuality are often muddled, leading to confusion and sometimes even outright misconceptions. We may worry about our desirability or the state of our relationships, but it's important to clarify what intimacy truly means. Intimacy is not solely about physical attraction or sexual activity—it's about the deep sense of closeness and connectedness we feel in our relationships, whether or not a physical component is involved.

Emotional intimacy occurs when we care deeply about someone else, feel a sense of trust, share similar values, and can express ourselves freely. This kind of intimacy is the foundation of close relationships, where we feel valued and connected to our partner on intellectual and emotional levels. Physical intimacy, on the other hand, is one way to express our sexuality through acts of touch—like hugging, cuddling, hand-holding, and sexual intercourse.

Intimate relationships, whether they are romantic or platonic, are crucial for our sense of connection and well-being. Terms like Besties, Ride-Or-Dies, BFFs, and Tribe capture the importance of these bonds. When we feel loved, seen, and appreciated—and when we see, love, and appreciate others—our mental and physical health improves. These connections nourish our souls and provide a sense of belonging that is essential at every stage of life.

> In an intimate relationship, you feel valued and connected.

Intimacy, at its core, is based on honesty and communication. While physical intimacy can be enhanced by these qualities, it's possible to engage in sexual activity without them. However, for those who seek to sustain or cultivate true intimacy—both platonic and physical—clarity on one's internal framework is vital. Knowing what you value, what you need, and what you're willing to give in a relationship is the foundation for deep, lasting connections.

As we age, many of us find that making new friends and sustaining old friendships becomes more challenging. We may carry the psychological weight of past pain or grief from relationship conflicts, divorce, illness, or death. These experiences can lead to issues with trust and commitment, making us less emotionally available. Yet, clarity on our emerging third chapter can help mitigate or overcome these challenges. Intimate friendships, in turn, can support us as we continue on a healthy, fulfilling path.

EXERCISES: CULTIVATING AND SUSTAINING INTIMACY

REFLECT ON YOUR CURRENT RELATIONSHIPS:

Take some time to reflect on the relationships in your life. Which ones bring you a deep sense of connection and intimacy? Are there any relationships that feel strained or distant? Consider what steps you can take to nurture or heal these connections, whether through open communication, spending quality time together, or expressing appreciation for one another.

CLARIFY YOUR NEEDS AND VALUES:

Intimacy requires clarity—both within yourself and in your relationships. Spend some time journaling about what you value most in your intimate relationships. What do you need from your close connections, and what are you willing to offer in return? This clarity can guide you in cultivating deeper, more fulfilling relationships.

CREATE A SELF-LOVE RITUAL:

Choose one relationship where you feel comfortable practicing deeper communication. Start by expressing something you value about the relationship, and then share a need or desire you have for strengthening your connection. Encourage the other person to do the same. This practice can help build trust and emotional intimacy.

INTENTION

I choose to nurture intimacy in my relationships, cultivating honesty, communication, and clarity. I honor the deep connections in my life and seek to sustain them with love and appreciation.

Your Intention for Turn #10:

NOTES

turn 11

SHOWING UP

As elder women, we first need to step inward before we can confidently step out into the world. And step out we will! After all, while we may live alone, we do not live in isolation. However, when we do step out after embracing aging with wisdom and wonder, we are likely to have changed in ways that others may not expect or even understand. The question then arises: How do we introduce—or re-introduce—ourselves as we are today?

We owe it to ourselves to show up authentically, to present our true selves rather than crafting personas to fit each person or situation we encounter. Many of us have spent a lifetime employing that tactic, what Brené Brown refers to as "armor." It's a protective mechanism, but it's also exhausting. The whole purpose of aging with wisdom and wonder is to help us break free from that pattern, to find stillness and clarity as we identify our essential values, goals, and directions. Because let's be clear: we're not done yet!

The benefit of living authentically is profound and multifaceted. When you live authentically, you experience a deep sense of inner peace and fulfillment because your actions, decisions, and relationships are aligned with your true self. This alignment fosters self-respect and confidence, as you no longer feel the need to conform to others' expectations or societal norms that don't resonate with you.

> Authenticity fosters resilience for a happier, healthier life.

Living authentically also strengthens your relationships, as it encourages genuine connections based on honesty and mutual respect. People who value and appreciate you for who you truly are become your circle, creating a supportive and empowering community around you.

Moreover, authenticity empowers you to navigate life's challenges with greater resilience. When you are grounded in your values and true to yourself, you are less swayed by external pressures or the opinions of others. This stability allows you to make decisions with clarity and purpose, leading to a more meaningful and fulfilling life.

Ultimately, living authentically enhances your overall well-being, reducing stress and anxiety caused by the effort of maintaining a facade or pleasing others. It enables you to live with integrity, where your outer life reflects your inner truth, leading to a life of greater joy, connection, and empowerment.

Gloria Steinem once said, "The art of living is not controlling what happens to us, but using what happens to us." As elder women, we have an abundance of experiences, lessons, and insights from our prior lives to draw upon as we concoct our next chapter. But if we fall short of living authentically, we risk surrendering our power to others, allowing them to define and control us once again.

As we explored in Turn #10, the settings and people with whom we choose to show up may evolve from previous patterns. Perhaps our tolerance for certain groups or environments has reached its limits, or maybe we feel emboldened to explore new activities and meet new people. The possibilities are endless, but it's crucial that the choices we make align with our essential selves.

Showing up authentically means being true to who you are now, not who you were or who others expect you to be. It means honoring your growth, your wisdom, and your right to live fully and freely in this new phase of life. This is your time to shine, to step out into the world as the powerful elder you've become.

EXERCISES: EMBRACING AUTHENTICITY AND SHOWING UP

REFLECT ON YOUR AUTHENTIC SELF:

Take some time to reflect on who you are now. How have you changed from the person you were before? What values, goals, and directions are most important to you at this stage of life? Write down your reflections to gain clarity on how you want to show up in the world.

PRACTICE AUTHENTICITY IN SMALL STEPS:

Choose one situation or relationship where you feel comfortable practicing authenticity. Start by being more open about your true thoughts, feelings, or desires, and notice how it feels to show up as your authentic self. Gradually, expand this practice to other areas of your life.

REINTRODUCE YOURSELF TO THE WORLD:

Consider how you might reintroduce yourself to others as a wise and wonderous elder. This could be in social settings, family gatherings, or even in your online presence. Think about how you want to present your authentic self and take steps to do so, whether it's through your words, actions, or the choices you make.

INTENTION

I choose to show up authentically, embracing who I am as a wise and wondrous elder. I honor my growth, my wisdom, and my right to live fully and freely in this new phase of life.

Your Intention for Turn #11:

NOTES

turn 12

WISDOM AND WONDER CEREMONY

With millions of women entering, or about to enter, their third chapters, there has never been a better time to reflect and reclaim our power. As powerful elders, we have the opportunity to step fully into our wisdom, embrace our experiences, and celebrate the transformation that comes with this new phase of life. We can celebrate this renewal, agency, and direction now and in days to come.

Wise and wonderous elders can find and be teachers, cultivating new networks of like-minded women to build strength, solidarity, and connections. By being proactive about our choices, building daily wellness practices for mind and body, and focusing on what is nurturing and healthy, we set a strong foundation for this journey.

Throughout our lives, we mark significant transitions with ceremonies and rituals that honor the passage from one stage to the next. From birth to marriage, and even the passing into the afterlife, we gather to celebrate, acknowledge, and witness these pivotal moments. Think of the joyous celebrations that mark a birth or a birthday, the solemnity and beauty of a wedding, or the reflective remembrance of a memorial service. Each of these rituals serves to anchor us, both individually and collectively, in the flow of life's journey.

> May you find clarity and wisdom and your third age unfolds.

The transition into our third chapter is no different. It is a time of great spiritual, emotional, and psychological growth—a time to celebrate life, harvest the wisdom of our years of experiences and share our legacy and stories with others. This phase of life, like those before it, deserves to be marked with intention and reverence. An intentional ceremony provides the space to do just that, offering a moment to witness, honor, and celebrate the rich tapestry of your life and the new chapter you are beginning.

Having now journeyed through this Wisdom and Wonder process, it is your time to celebrate! A ceremony witnesses, honors, and celebrates you as you step into your own version of the Wise Woman archetype. This ceremony taps into your attributes of clarity, compassion, healing, and transformation, which you've explored throughout this process.

SETTING THE SCENE

Consider creating a sacred space that surrounds and holds you with the elements—fire (sun and candle), earth (rocks, trees, fallen leaves), water (ocean, stream, fountain), and air (wind, feathers, and breath). If you used totems, stones, or scents in your sacred space during this journey, consider bringing those to the ceremony as well.

Gather those intimates who support you most in this evolution and who will stand by you in the months and years ahead. You may choose to lead the ceremony yourself, or you may work with an officiant who understands the significance of this moment. Music, whether live or recorded, can heighten the sacredness of the ceremony. You might include a small drumming or music circle where your invitees join in chanting or rhythmic sounds, bringing greater unity to the group.

Dress in clothes that best represent your fabulous self, and encourage those invited to do the same. Alternatively, you might choose to wear something with deep personal significance, such as a gown or a garment that symbolizes your journey. And of course, plan on a crown—you've earned it!

THE CEREMONY

Begin by bathing before the ceremony to underscore the cleansing of your past as you move forward to meet your future. This ritual of purification sets the stage for stepping into your new role with clarity and intention.

Consider using the intentions you created for each Turn as the basis of the ceremony. If you are working with an officiant, she might ask you directly, "And what would you have us understand about accepting the full circle of life?" This would continue for each of the Turns, similar to how Khalil Gibran introduces wisdom in The Prophet.

Depending on the length of the ceremony, you might invite your guests to reflect on the truths you've summarized in each intention. This creates a collective space for acknowledging the wisdom and clarity you've gained.

DECLARING YOUR RENEWAL, AGENCY, AND DIRECTION

Take a moment during the ceremony to declare your renewal, agency, and direction as a wise and wonderous elder. Speak or write about the path you've chosen, the values you uphold, and the intentions you carry forward into this new phase of life. This declaration serves as a powerful affirmation of your commitment to living authentically and fully as you step into your third chapter.

INVITING BLESSINGS

Invite blessings into your life, whether through prayer or meditation or by simply opening your heart to the possibilities ahead. You might call upon the wisdom of your ancestors, the support of loved ones, or the strength of the natural elements to guide and protect you on your journey.

CONCLUDING WITH A BLESSING

Conclude the ceremony with a blessing that resonates deeply with you. A simple one might be: "We have gathered here to support and acknowledge the wisdom of [your name], who has learned to walk in her truth, in her own way, having gained strength by acknowledging the power and wisdom of her life's journey. May each of you find clarity and wisdom as your third age unfolds. Blessings be."

Finish the ceremony with an exchange of gifts, such as teas, journals, crystals, apples, or small evergreen or succulent plants. This symbolizes the exchange of support, nourishment, and growth that will continue in your life as a wise and wonderous elder.

Finally, gather afterward in a potluck to underscore the vitality and nourishment that the community provides. This shared meal is a celebration of the connections you've made and the journey you've undertaken.

NOTES

Farewell
WHERE WISDOM MEETS WONDER

Dear Wise and Wonderous Elder,

As you close this workbook, take a moment to sit quietly to reflect on the incredible journey you've undertaken. Consider the wisdom you've uncovered, the truths you've embraced, and the connections you've strengthened—both with others and within yourself. This has been no ordinary journey; this has been a reclamation, a celebration, a profound step into your third chapter with power and intention.

Through each Turn, you've peeled back layers of societal expectations, outdated beliefs, and self-imposed limitations. You've delved into the essence of who you are, rediscovering your strength, your resilience, and your ability to live authentically. You've reconnected with the sacredness of your experiences, honoring the life you've lived and the person you've become.

But let's be clear—this journey isn't about becoming someone new. It's about embracing the woman you've always been, but perhaps haven't fully acknowledged. It's about stepping into the light with all your wisdom, your scars, your stories, and your joys. It's about showing up in the world as the vibrant, powerful, and wise woman you are.

You've explored what it means to live mindfully, to sustain intimacy, to honor yourself, and to navigate your beliefs with clarity. You've reconnected with Gaia and celebrated simplicity, and now, you stand ready to step into the world with renewed agency and direction. The ceremony you've planned is not just a ritual—it's a declaration. A declaration that you are here, that you matter, and that your voice, your wisdom, and your presence will light the way for others.

As you move forward, carry with you the intentions, the insights, and the profound sense of self that you've cultivated. Know that this journey doesn't end with the final page of this workbook. It continues in every choice you make, in every interaction, in every moment of stillness and reflection. You are a Wise and Wonderous Elder—part of a growing network of women who are reclaiming their power and rewriting the narrative of aging.

So here's to you, wise woman. Here's to your strength, your grace, and your courage to embrace the fullness of life. Here's to the community you've built and the legacy you will leave behind. May your third chapter be filled with laughter, love, and the deep satisfaction of knowing that you are living your truth, every single day.

Welcome to the wonder of aging in power. You've earned your crown.
With love, respect, and a shared sense of purpose,

Jen

WHERE WISDOM MEETS *Wonder*

A Workbook of Renewal, Agency, and Direction

SUMMARY AND READING RESOURCES

The Where Wisdom Meets Wonder workbook guides women along a journey of renewal, agency, and direction. The methodology invites women to consider past practices and habits to see if these were truly their own or if society has led them down pathways that were not in their best interest—particularly as she has aged.

Where Wisdom Meets Wonder is designed to be practical and actionable, and strives to meet women where they are today and support them towards a more meaningful, intentional third chapter.

The methodology is built on my research and analysis. In keeping with life's cyclical nature, each segment of this workbook is called a "Turn." Below are brief descriptions of each Turn in the workbook, along with selected reading resources that informed them.

CREATIVE EXPRESSION AND THE JOURNEY INWARD

A sacred space can facilitate the journey inward, creating a sanctuary where you can retreat, reflect, and recharge. Statues, totems, crystals, incense, or other elements imbue a sacred space with meaning and intention. What matters most is that these resonate with you and support your wisdom and wonder journey.

Castleman, Michael, The New Healing Herbs: Revised and Updated. Bantam Books, November 2002

Estés, Dr. Clarissa Pinkola. The Power of the Crone: Myths and Stories of the Wise Woman Archetype. Sounds True, May 2011.

Simmons, Robert and Naisha Ahsian, The Book of Stones: Who They Are and What They Teach. North Atlantic Books, January 2015.
The website Spirit Animal has a comprehensive set of the significance of animal totems. https://www.spiritanimal.info/

TURN #1—OWNING OUR AGING: OPENING THE EXPLORATION

This Turn challenges the traditional perception of aging and the words we use to refer to aging—particularly for ourselves. Collectively, elder women can claim labels and use these for power, wisdom, and grace. It encourages women to embrace aging as a time of transformation and self-discovery, focusing on wisdom, and continuous growth. The journey into the later years is framed not as an end, but as a powerful new beginning.

Applewhite, Ashton. This Chair Rocks: A Manifesto Against Ageism. Self-published 2016.

Jeannette Encinias. Silver (For Suzy). https://medium.com/mindful/a-poem-to-ease-aging-cfaa560d9cb8

TURN #2—ACCEPTING THE FULL LIFE CYCLE: EMBRACING THE PROGRESSION OF LIFE

Turn #2 focuses on accepting the natural progression of aging, recognizing the wisdom and beauty that come with each stage of life. It encourages the reader to embrace their crone years as a time of reflection, growth, and deep connection to the cycles of life.

Bolen, Jean Shinoda. Crones Don't Whine: Concentrated Wisdom for Juicy Women (Inspiration for Mature Women, Aging Gracefully, Divine Feminine, Gift for Women). Conari Press, 2021

...Goddess in Older Women. Harper Paperbacks, 2014.

TURN #3—LIVING MINDFULLY: RECLAIMING PRESENCE

This Turn explores the shift from a busy, worry-filled life to one of mindfulness and intentional living. It highlights the importance of being fully present in the moment, setting boundaries, and creating a life that aligns with one's values and desires.

Dispenza, Joe, Breaking The Habit of Being Yourself: How to Lose Your Mind and Create a New One. Hay House, LLC, February 2013.

Richardson, Cheryl, The Art of Extreme Self-Care: 12 Practical and Inspiring Ways to Love Yourself More. Hay House, LLC, November 2019.

TURN #4—RESPECTING COMPASSIONATELY: LISTENING WITH THE HEART

Turn #4 delves into the practice of compassionate listening, both towards others and within oneself. Here we emphasize the healing power of listening without judgment, offering empathy and kindness in conversations, and cultivating a more compassionate internal dialogue.

Clear, James. Be Ruthless about What You Ignore. https://jamesclear.com/3-2-1/november-16-2023

Cohen, Andrea S, Practicing the Art of Compassionate Listening. Compassionate Listening Project, July 2022.

Guzmán, Mónica, I Never Thought of It That Way. BenBella Books, March 2022.

TURN #5—HONORING SELF: NOURISHING FROM WITHIN

This Turn focuses on the importance of self-honoring through nurturing activities and positive habits. It encourages the reader to prioritize self-care, embrace her strengths and limitations, and create a life that supports her well-being and celebrates who they are today and in the years to come.

Blackie, Sharon. Hagitude: If Women Rose Rooted. September Publishing, 2020.
..., The Enchanted Life: Unlocking the Magic of the Everyday. September Publishing, 2018.

Northrup M.D., Christiane, Goddesses Never Age: The Secret Prescription for Radiance, Vitality, and Well-Being. Hay House, Inc., 2016.

TURN #6—LOVING SELF: EMBRACING THE FULLNESS OF WHO YOU ARE

Turn #6 explores the concept of self-love, emphasizing the need to accept, nurture, and value oneself. It addresses the importance of healing past wounds, practicing self-compassion, and deepening one's relationship with self-love as a vital part of aging in wisdom and wonder.

Curran, Thomas. The Perfection Trap: Embracing the Power of Good Enough. London, 2023.

Lamar, Jay, Ed. Old Enough: Southern Women Artists and Writers on Creativity and Aging. New South Books, May 2024.

TURN #7—APPRECIATING SIMPLICITY: EMBRACING WHAT TRULY MATTERS

This Turn highlights the desire to simplify life as one enters one's third chapter, focusing on decluttering, downsizing, and living in alignment with what is most essential. It encourages the reader to appreciate simplicity in all areas of life, creating a foundation of clarity, connection, and peace.

Becker, Joshua, Things That Matter: Overcoming Distraction to Pursue a More Meaningful Life. Waterbrook Publishing, 2022.

Nestle and Nourish has practical downsizing challenges: https://nourishandnestle.com/

TURN #8—LOVING GAIA: RECONNECTING WITH OUR EARTH MOTHER

Turn #8 emphasizes the importance of living in harmony with the earth, recognizing the interconnectedness between personal well-being and environmental stewardship. It encourages the reader to adopt sustainable practices, reconnect with nature, and contribute to the healing of Gaia.

Johnson, Bea, Zero Waste Home: The Ultimate Guide to Simplifying Your Life by Reducing Your Waste. Penguin Publishing, 2016.

Kimmerer, Robin Wall, Braiding Sweetgrass: Indigenous Wisdom, Scientific Knowledge, and the Teaching of the Plants. Milkweed Editions, 2013.

Wangari Maathai, Replenishing the Earth: Spiritual Values for Healing Ourselves and the World. Doubleday Religion, 2010.

TURN #9—NAVIGATING BELIEFS: CULTIVATING CLARITY AND SELF-ORIENTATION

This Turn focuses on the process of navigating personal beliefs in a polarized world, encouraging the reader to gain clarity on their values and live authentically. It highlights the importance of cultivating tools to manage conflict, protecting one's well-being, and staying connected to the sacred.

Brown, Brené, Braving the Wilderness: The Quest for True Belonging and the Courage to Stand Alone. Random House, 2017.

TURN #10—SUSTAINING INTIMACY: NURTURING CONNECTIONS

This Turn delves into the nuanced topic of sustaining intimacy, emphasizing the importance of connection, honesty, and communication in relationships as we age.

Bildtgård, Torbjörn and Peter Öberg, Intimacy and Ageing. Policy Press 2018

Walker, Alice. In Search of Our Mothers' Gardens: Womanist Prose. Houghton Mifflin Harcourt Press, October 1983.

TURN #11—SHOWING UP: EMBRACING AUTHENTICITY

Turn #11 focuses on the importance of showing up authentically as a conscious crone, embracing the changes that come with this new phase of life, and stepping out into the world with confidence.

Maran, Meredith. The New Old Me: My Late-Life Reinvention. Blue Rider Press, May 2014.

Ott, Joanne Sienko, The Crone Archetype: Women Reclaim Their Authentic Self by Resonating with Crone Images. https://sophia.stkate.edu/ma_hhs/17. 2011

Thomas, Ann. The Women We Become: Myths, Folktales, and Stories About Growing Older. Volcano Press, January 2004.

TURN #12—WISDOM AND WONDER CEREMONY

Turn #12 considers how we traditionally celebrate life passages, tying our aging ceremony into a broader narrative of marking significant transitions with reverence and intention. This intentionality reinforces the importance of celebrating this powerful moment in a way that honors the journey and transformation you've experienced.

Pipher, Mary, Women Rowing North: Navigating Life's Currents and Flourishing As We Age. Bloomsbury Publishing, March 2020.

Nussbaum, Martha C. and Saul Levmore, Aging Thoughtfully: Conversations about Retirement, Romance, Wrinkles, and Regret. Oxford University Press, November 2017.

O'Donohue, John. For a New Beginning. https://sacompassion.net/poem-for-a-new-beginning-by-john-odonohue/

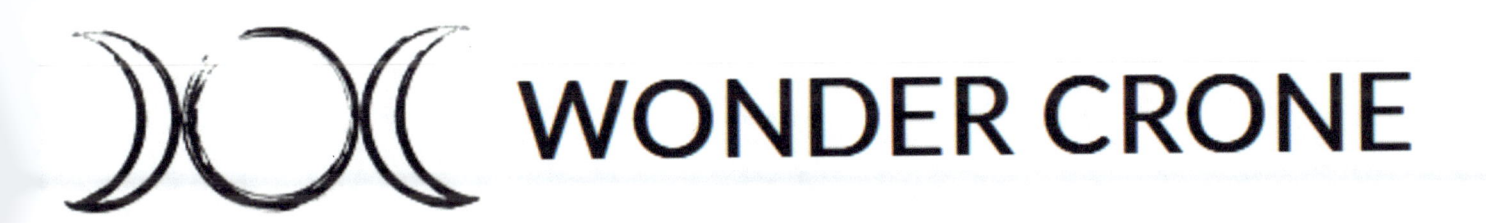

WONDER CRONE

Made in the USA
Columbia, SC
08 February 2025